Then and Now

Part II

Bonnie Baker

Christian Living Books, Inc.
Largo, MD

Copyright © 2013 Bonnie Baker

All rights reserved under the international copyright law. No part of this book may be reproduced or transmitted in any form or by any means, electronic or mechanical, including photocopying, recording, or by any information storage and retrieval system, without the express, written permission of the author or publisher. The exception is reviewers, who may quote brief passages in a review.

ISBN 978-1-56229-818-0

Christian Living Books, Inc.
Largo, Maryland
ChristianLivingBooks.com

Printed in the United States of America

Unless otherwise indicated, Scripture quotations are taken from the Holy Bible, King James Version, Cambridge, 1769.

Scripture quotations marked (NIV) are taken from the Holy Bible, New International Version®, NIV®. Copyright © 1973, 1978, 1984, 2011 by Biblica, Inc.™ Used by permission of Zondervan. All rights reserved worldwide. The "NIV" and "New International Version" are trademarks registered in the United States Patent and Trademark Office by Biblica, Inc.™.

Dedication

I would like to dedicate this book to my Lord and Savior, Jesus Christ, for inspiring me to write Part II of *Then and Now*, my life story. To my husband and children, all my natural brothers and sisters, all my loved ones that have gone on to be with the Lord, my nine children, my parents, my grandparents, my father-in-law, my brothers and sisters-in-law, the late Apostle Charles O. Miles, Dad and Mother Poole, my memories and love still remain the same. I will never forget you.

Contents

Foreword vii
Preface ix
Acknowledgments xi

Then…

Chapter 1 – From the Beginning 1
Chapter 2 – Looking for Love 5
Chapter 3 – We Overcome by the Word of Our Testimony 11
Chapter 4 – Silent No More 17
Chapter 5 – Don't Go Back 35

…and Now

Chapter 6 – A Call from God. 45
Chapter 7 – Visions and Dreams 53
Chapter 8 – The Four Seasons 57
Chapter 9 – Wake Up and Call on Jesus 67
Chapter 10 – My Family and Their Words 73
About the Author 83

Foreword

In *Then and Now, Part II*, Evangelist Bonnie Baker continues to share her testimony about how God has personally delivered her and set her free. She exposes the tricks and devices of the devil and declares that God will do the same for you. God will be to you whatever you allow Him to be (Savior, Deliverer, Healer, Protector, Friend, etc.).

I've known Evangelist Bonnie Baker for many years. She has a servant's heart, serving faithfully on several auxiliaries at International Gospel Center.

I'm confident that this book will be a blessing to you.

Pastor Marvin N. Miles
International Gospel Center
Ecorse, Michigan

Preface

Minister Bonnie Baker and I met over 30 years ago at the International Gospel Center. Ministers Dean and Bonnie had recently become engaged and were in the process of planning their wedding. We were introduced by a mutual friend, who suggested to her that I could help with the planning of her wedding. From that day, we became the best of friends. We are both from Alabama. From time to time, we would visit each other when home visiting our parents.

I am so proud of my friend, Bonnie, and glad to be her friend. I knew something was different about her the day we meet. Bonnie has the gifts of many colors, one of which is the gift hospitality. She loves to invite you to her house to fellowship. She prepares awesome meals and feeds you until you are filled to capacity. Bonnie then sends you home with a full – and I mean full – carry-out bag.

This is a powerful woman of God that walks and preaches the word of God. She preaches from her soul. I have seen her go through many trials and tribulations and come out of each one. Each time she ministers, the anointing on her life increases from on high.

Life carried Minister Bonnie to places that I am sure she would have loved to have skipped over, like all of us. Nevertheless, she scaled the rough side of her mountain; she has wandered through her wilderness; she has fallen into deep valleys! God delivered her out with triumphant victory. You see, you don't know *all* of her story. James 1:3 says, "Knowing that the testing of your faith produces patience." I have seen patience in her like never before.

Her life story tells how she overcame death many, many times. Minister Baker's first book was awesome. Anyone who read it can attest to that. You couldn't put it down. It blessed thousands and thousands of people.

This woman of God has a lot to share with this lost generation. Her second book, *Surviving Your Worst Fear* is a must read. You have nothing to fear but fear itself. Minister Baker, continue to let God use you in everything you do. I am confident that this book will be a great blessing to all who read it. Let go of the past; that was THEN. Embrace the NOW because it will lead to your future.

Your friend and sister in Christ
Minister Gloria Burton

Acknowledgments

To Jesus Christ, who is the head of my life, the one who saved me and set me free from all my bondage. To all the ones who stood by me and believed in me: Pastors Frederick and Hattie Hopkins, Pastor Marvin N. Miles, First Lady Carolyn Miles, Mother Luvenia Miles, my mother-in-law, all my family, my friends, my church family, all my god children, thanks for all your love and support down through the years and years counting. I love you much. Last, but not least, to my one and only, special and sweet GRANDSON, little Ivan: Granny loves you.

Special thanks to Event Photography Images by Kevin Bean and Photography by Pat McDowell.

1
From the Beginning

I grew up in the small town of Vredenburgh, Alabama (which only has a population of 500), to Jack and Clara Richardson. I was the seventh of ten children. I had seven brothers: Jack, Burlee, James, Clarence, Armie Lee, Alexander, and Nathaniel; and two sisters: Barbara and Emma, who was also known as Hattie. Jack and Clarence are no longer with us.

Because Vredenburgh was so small, everyone knew everyone else. We walked everywhere that we needed to go. My parents picked cotton, went fishing, and made lots of syrup. We also grew peaches, pecans, corn, beans, okra, greens, sweet potatoes, and sugar cane. There was no shortage of food to eat. We could choose from the pigs and chickens we raised as well as from the fish that Daddy and Mommy would catch. Then, there were the eggs the hens laid, from time to time.

My father was a hard worker. He worked at the saw mill. My mother was a stay-at-home mom. We were living well for back in the day. We owned a television, a line phone, and an outhouse in the rear of our house. Some of our neighbors had to walk a long way to use the bathroom. We didn't have to do that.

From the age of two months to the age of twelve years, the devil tried to kill me. As an infant, he attacked me with double pneumonia. I stayed in the hospital for two months before the

Lord healed me. Also, when my fourth grade class went on a field trip to the beach in Pensacola, Florida, I almost drowned to death and had to receive mouth-to-mouth resuscitation in order to be revived. This was the origin of many of the fears that I described in *Surviving Your Worst Fear*. It took me years to be delivered from the fear of drowning, as well as, many other fears.

The Belt

There are some things that you never forget. I remember the stove we had in the kitchen. I had to make the fire every morning before Mommy could start cooking breakfast. If I overslept and my mother woke up before I had made the fire, I got the belt. It felt as if a fire had been lit on my backside. In fact, I received the most whippings of all of my siblings.

At age twelve, I got whipped so badly that I thought I would die. My school was selling hot dogs to make money for a field trip and I had asked for thirty cents to buy two hot dogs. When I didn't receive it, I stole a ten dollar bill. If I had gotten the thirty cents, I wouldn't have taken the ten dollar bill. I knew stealing was wrong but, I took it anyway. I was only trying to take a dollar, but, I just grabbed the first bill I saw.

I was living it up, buying everyone at school a hot dog. That was my downfall. My sister, Emma, and my best friend told Mommy that I had been spending a lot of money at school. I paid dearly for those actions. To this day, I have the marks on my back which serve as a reminder to me about the wrong that I did.

Chapter 1 • From the Beginning

I stayed mad for days. I got pass that and right back into something else. The devil was trying to take me out at an early age. I wanted to run away from home but had nowhere to go. I detail my childhood in my first book, *Then and Now*.

At age fifteen, God saved me but, I didn't have enough power to stay saved. I went back to doing what I liked to do and that was dancing. I loved dancing. At age sixteen, I won Miss Vredenburgh High, which made me the "queen" of my school. There were two runner ups. WOW! That was big for me after everything I had already been through. Of course, as queen of the school, I received a lot of attention from boys. I yielded and enjoyed it all.

Our parents were very strict on us; we couldn't go anywhere. On Sunday, everyone in the neighborhood would meet at the neighborhood club, The Green End. Daddy and Mommy would let us go, every now and then; but, we had to be back in the house by 5:00 PM and in bed by 6:30 PM.

After all that I had to go through, I can see the hand of God on my life – for such a time as this. I was always trying to find a way to sneak out. I was so afraid to tell anyone that I liked a boy. I knew that my Daddy would put the lock down on me. So, I start talking secretly to one of my schoolmates. We started liking each other. Well, that's what I thought. However, we did not tell anyone we were talking to one another.

One day, out of the blue, he asked me to marry him. I said "Yes" so quickly that I caught him off guard. We wondered how we were going to tell my parents that he asked me to marry him.

I thought, *I'm not even supposed to have a boyfriend. Now, I am talking about marrying someone!*

My oldest sister, Barbara, was home from Detroit for a little while. I told her about my engagement. She helped me break the news to my parents. It did not sit with them too well. My Daddy didn't say a word. Mommy said, "WHAT?"

I was so sad as I waited days for my parents to say something. Then, one Sunday evening, my parents began to talk to me.

They asked a lot of questions: "Does he have a job? Where are you going to live? How will you get around?"

They looked at me, with tears in their eyes – I had tears in my eyes, too – and said, "Okay." After that, he asked them for my hand in marriage.

2
Looking for Love

We finally got married. My husband moved us all the way to Pensacola, Florida. That turned out to be the biggest mistake I had ever made. I got married at the age of eighteen just so that I could get out of the house. I had to pay for that mistake, over and over again. My husband told me that he loved me. However, he was cheating on me with everybody that he could. He did not even want me to leave the house, not even to go to the store.

I had to eat watermelon for breakfast, lunch, and dinner. All day – and sometimes, all night – I waited for him to come home and bring me some food to eat. I got very sick from eating all that watermelon. I believe that was the origin of bad eating habits which continued later on in life. I was very thin. In fact, I was almost anorexic.

He would start a fight whenever I asked him about why he was gone for so long. That was the beginning of the physical abuse. He would beat me and threaten me so that I would not tell anyone. All I wanted was to be happy and to be loved.

Had my Daddy or brothers known about the abuse, there would have been trouble. My Daddy told my husband that if he ever reached a point at which he didn't want me anymore or got tired of me to bring me back home.

To that, my husband replied, "That is not going to happen. I love her." My heart dropped after he said that. I had to bribe him to let me catch the bus to go see my parents. He did let me go, but he only allowed me to go a few times.

My brother, James, found out that my husband was seeing a woman in our little trailer park. When James told me, I didn't want to hear it because I loved my husband. James told me to leave him and go back home to our parent's house. I didn't want to go back home again. I was very sad, hurt, and angry. I had wasted the last year of high school and eight months of my life with a man that was not true. I wondered why he married me in the first place. I questioned my *own* decision and wondered why I had gotten married.

After eight months of abuse and loneliness, I got up enough nerve to leave him. I moved to Michigan to live with Barbara. A few months after I got there, I began to meet all the wrong people. You see, the devil was still trying to kill me.

Please Don't Let Me Drown!

The first man I met in Michigan was a drug user. I almost got hooked on drugs, myself. I used to have headaches and he would give me a pill that I thought was for headaches. It would make me see mirages. One night, he gave me two pills. Now, that almost took me out. I began to see a river… right in front of me. I just panicked, and I began to scream and holler. Barbara had to almost carry me upstairs to put me in the bed.

I was screaming and tears were streaming down my face, "I can't go up the stairs. I am about to drown. Help me. Help

Chapter 2 • Looking for Love

me. Barbara, please don't let me fall into this river and die!" I was pulling on her, hitting her, and fighting her. *That* was a night to remember.

One day, I had another headache. When my boyfriend asked me whether or not I wanted another pill, I told him, "No! No! No!"

"I know what kind of medicine you need," he said. "I won't give you another one of those. I know you can't handle them."

So, I believed him and took the pill he gave me. We went to the gas station to get gas. While he was inside the store, that pill began to work. I opened the car door and began to walk across Livernois Street in Detroit. I walked right into on-coming traffic, during rush hour.

A man jumped out of his car and said, "Lady! Lady! What are you doing? You are about to be hit by on-coming traffic!" He walked me back to the gas station.

I was totally out of it. I didn't know where I was or who I was. My boyfriend ran out of the gas station, grabbed me, exchanged words with the man that walked me to safety, put me in the car, and drove off. I still didn't know what had happened, where I was, or who I was.

I began to holler, "Don't drive into that river." Clearly, I was not in my right mind. It took me days to come down off of that high.

Sometime later, my boyfriend confessed to giving me another one of those pills. I didn't really remember anything about the incident at the gas station. I was so shocked when he told me about what happened. Thanks to the prayers that went up on my behalf, I am in my right mind, today. My mother was praying; my grandmother was praying; my sister, Pastor Hopkins (Emma) and her best friend were praying. Everyone that knew how to pray was praying for me, all the time.

Family and people – of many faiths – agree that prayer is a powerful tool; it does work. It was helpful to feel supported and know that they were praying for me. I did feel better… even in my sin. They prayed to God – over and over and over again – to "save me." They didn't stop praying until I got saved.

> *Thou wilt keep him in perfect peace, whose mind is stayed on Thee: because he trusteth in Thee.* (Isaiah 26:3)

Knowing that my family was concerned about and praying for me really made a difference in my life. I am a living witness that praying for someone helps them – even when they do not know you are praying.

> *Confess your faults one to another, and pray one for another, that ye may be healed. The effectual fervent prayer of a righteous man availeth much.* (James 5:16)

But God

Shortly after that, my boyfriend was shot dead in his driveway. I was supposed to be with him that night. I probably would have gotten shot, too. But God!! I cannot say it enough times: prayer really changes things in your life.

After going through the hurt of losing him, I began to move on… I was looking for love, again. I was in the big city and wanted to make it big. I thought it was good to be with the

Chapter 2 • Looking for Love

big and bad people. I ended up with the wrong crowd, every time. I felt like my life was going around and around, like a roller coaster.

I was so empty. I was searching, high and low, for something to fill that emptiness. There is a vacuum, shaped hole inside of all of us that only God can fill. No attempt to fill that void another way will be successful. I was looking for love in all the wrong places. I know it sounds cliché but it's the truth. While I was looking, I met this pimp. This man was the worst one of them all. I wrote a lot about this in *Then and Now*. He later became my second husband. I fell deeply in love with him. At least, I thought I did. I would do anything to be with him. It would just do something to me whenever he said, "I love you." And, I believed him.

My family warned me, "He is not the one." They didn't like it when I married him.

3
We Overcome by the Word of our Testimony

I thank God for letting me write my life story, *Then and Now*. That book has become a blessing to the body of Christ, as well as, to the world. I continue to receive numerous letters, phone calls, and texts attesting to that fact. Whether it's face to face, one on one, or in a group setting, many tell me their stories. They share testimonies involving abuse, rape, drugs, alcohol, gambling, incarceration, depression and even, suicide – all the things that I had been through and even some things that I had not been through which isn't much.

I could never have imagined that God would take what I went through and use it for His glory – using it to set people free. The *Now* part of my life began over thirty one years ago. By the power of God, many have been set free from unforgiveness, pain, hurt, abuse, alcoholism, gambling, and much more. I cannot even tell you how many people have told me that *some* part of the book hit home with them in their lives.

A Pastor confessed, "I was raped by my father."

An Evangelist confessed, "I was abused by my uncles."

A choir member confessed, "My cousin abused me for years." Many confessed that their mother's boyfriend abused them.

A friend confessed, "I have to forgive my father for what he did to me."

People at various churches I ministered in, men and women in high places, high ranking officials, teachers, homemakers, boys, and girls were all speaking up, "It happened to me, too. And now, I can finally deal with it."

Many letters touched me. Different ones began to tell me what they had been through. But one letter inspired me; it reminded me of myself. It was from one of my daughter's friends. They were doing a project on date abuse for one of their college courses. My daughter brought in one of my books for her group to read.

Her friend said that she was mentally and physically abused by her father. The abuse led her to drinking alcohol, smoking weed and cigarettes, and ended up causing her to be very promiscuous – all at the age of 13. All she wanted to do was make money and have sex.

She ended up with a man that took power over her life and began to use – and abuse – her. He would beat her so badly until she was black and blue and had to play dead. After several years, she finally got up the courage to leave him.

He invited her to his birthday party but she didn't go. He ended up beating and killing a man that night. He is now serving a life sentence. She knew that could have been her. He probably would have beat and killed *her* that night. All this came from being abused by her father. She ended up almost dead. Her life went downhill. She resorted to dancing at strip clubs; she had a sugar daddy; and she lost a child.

Chapter 3 • We Overcome by the Word of our Testimony

She said that *Then and Now* fell into her hands at the perfect time. She went on to say that she believes it was meant for her to meet my daughter. She said my story gave her the inspiration and courage to move on in her life. She wanted to meet me and go to church with us and she did. I had a chance to talk with her and witness to her; she gave her life to the Lord. She also said she forgave her father. She forgave all the men that took advantage of her and who used and abused her when she was still a child.

One of my friends told me that her stepfather abused her, for years. She later found out that he had abused her children until they were in the fourth and fifth grade. Her grandmother was her baby sitter. Her stepfather would abuse the kids right there, in the home, and the grandmother didn't know it. It devastated the family. For years, she didn't want anything to do with her mother or her stepfather. To this day, the children still feel the effects of it. So many testimonies came in. So many people got free after *Then and Now* came out in 2003.

All Things Become New

One woman told me that she still has nightmares about being abused. From a little baby until she was ten years old, her stepfather sexually abused her. It messed her life up. She is still dealing with it. I told her that she is not alone. I told her that God will heal her but that she had to let it go and forgive.

> *And when ye stand praying, forgive, if ye have ought against any: that your Father also which is in heaven may forgive you your trespasses.* (Mark 11:25)

When you go through something like that, it makes you feel dirty. You are filled with shame, guilt and hurt. Day in and day out the question "WHY? WHY? WHY" is ringing in your head. But, you get no answers.

> *And be ye kind one to another, tenderhearted, forgiving one another, even as God for Christ's sake hath forgiven you.* (Ephesians 4:32)

When you give your heart to God, the devil constantly reminds you of what happened to you.

> *Therefore if any man be in Christ, he is a new creature: old things are passed away; behold, all things are become new.* (2 Corinthians 5:17)

You are washed in the blood. What happened to you has been washed in the blood, too. You have become new.

I began to travel to different states, preaching and telling my testimony, as the Lord led me. I let the people know that Jesus saves and will save you if you *want* to be saved. The Bible declares that confession is good for the soul because it is a condition of salvation.

> *That if thou shalt confess with thy mouth the Lord Jesus, and shalt believe in thine heart that God hath raised him from the dead, thou shalt be saved. For with the heart man believeth unto righteousness; and with the mouth confession is made unto salvation.* (Romans 10:9-10)

So, you have to confess and tell it. If you've been carrying abuse, rape, hate, hurt, or unforgiveness – and you want to be free – forgive all the people that abused you. Tell it; talk about it; don't keep holding it in; that only makes it worse.

Say, "No more. I've got to tell this so that I can be free!"

Chapter 3 • We Overcome by the Word of our Testimony

It doesn't matter how long it's been. It will always be in your mind. You will always remember it.

I Have to Tell This

This is the first time I am telling this. My family doesn't even know it. At a young age, I was sexually abused by a man and by a boy in Vredenburgh. This occurred many, many times in our garage, our outhouse, and on the nearby railroad track. This man would command me to come to the garage at a certain time of the evening. He would rape me over and over again. I was nine years old and *all* of this was against my will. I would try to yell, but he would put his hand over my mouth. I was afraid of him and didn't know what he would or could do to me or my family. I was just a little girl. It hurts to think about all of that, even now. Oh, my God. I *have* to tell this. The abuse continued for years until we moved to Beatrice, Alabama. I would see him at school. He would roll his eyes and stare at me in a mean… hateful… threating way. I was still afraid to tell anyone.

If you are going through the same thing or something like this, you've got to tell it. Don't put yourself through all of the hurt and pain that come with silence. Children, tell somebody you trust. If you told a loved one what was going on and they still let it happen, that is a case for God to deal with. I know how you feel. I was so afraid to tell anyone.

This man knew when my parents would go fishing and not be home. He would walk out, in front of our yard, so that I could see him. Then, he would point for me to come. It's like he had some type of spell over me. I never said anything to anyone. I didn't want to talk about it. I was too afraid. So, I just went on with my life. One day, it just came alive again in my mind. I kept it and never told anyone… until now. I was too afraid to tell Mommy or my sisters or anyone else in my family.

If you have never been through repeated sexual abuse, it's hard to understand. Demonic forces enable and empower abusers. Those forces are responsible for keeping the abused silent and for keeping the abuser undiscovered. It's strange that in a family of twelve, no one ever happened upon us or ever saw us. What forces keep parents and others blind?

Oftentimes, when victims tell their mothers about the abuse, mothers don't believe them… or at least they tell the children they don't believe them. If that child were to tell the parent *anything* else, the mother would not question it. However, when it comes to sexual abuse, parents often turn a blind eye or deaf ear.

Time and time again I've heard the testimony, "*No one* believed me."

4
Silent No More

I've been a member of International Gospel Center since the Lord saved me 31 years ago. One Sunday, Pastor Miles preached a message entitled, *Silent No More*. That message really hit home with me.

Pastor Miles just kept saying, "Silent No More. Tell it. The abused become abusive."

As I sat in the congregation, listening, I began to think back on what happened to me. Those things were always in the back of my mind. I never forgot them. From time to time, I would have nightmares about some of the things I'd been through. That Sunday, I lived it… all over again. Again and again, I would see the scenes, feel the feelings, and re-experience the pain.

With tears in my eyes, I wondered to myself, "Who can I share this with and not feel shame and hurt?"

I went to God. I had a talk with Him as if He was right there, sitting with me. My God has given me total victory over everything in my past. But, the memories were still there and would come to mind sometimes.

The message also took me back to the night when I was gang raped. For five hours, seven men raped me over and over and over again to the point at which I couldn't even walk. That was the worst, most horrifying night of my life. It was like someone putting a knife on the inside of your body and cutting you… over and over again… without any anesthesia… You can feel every rip and tear.

As the abuse continued, I began slipping in and out of consciousness. I felt that there was nothing else left for them to do to me *but* to kill me. So, I didn't want to live any more. I was bleeding from everywhere. I knew my body was messed up. They didn't even care one bit.

Help Me, Lord

My mind was racing with horrible thoughts. My eyes were almost shut from crying so hard from the pain and torture. I had no hope that I would see another day. Then, I decided that I didn't want to die. I decided to live. I knew how to pray. God had saved me at the age of fifteen but I turned my back on God and went back to doing what pleased me. At that moment, I couldn't pray aloud. I didn't have any strength left.

All I could think was "Help me! Help me. Help me, Lord!"

I went back and forth between wanting to live and wondering why they won't just kill me. "Why are they making me suffer? If they just kill me, I will feel no more pain. I am going to die at the age of nineteen."

One of the men held a gun to my head and said, "If you even open your mouth, I will blow you away. No one will ever find you. When we get through with you, no one will be able to recognize you." He went on to say, "You better act like you are enjoying this, too."

Chapter 4 • Silent No More

There I was, on the floor. They used me as if I were a dish rag. My body was wiping my own blood from the floor as I rolled over and over again in it! Oh, my God. It was horrifying. One man had one arm; another had the other arm; one man had one leg; another man had the other leg. One man had his hand over my mouth. One had a gun to my head. I could not move. All I could do was lay there and suffer… in pain.

Going into the fifth hour, I couldn't move. I thought they were going to kill me, finally. But… they kept coming back, raping me, over and over again as I lay there listening to them talk about it. They laughed and used all kinds of vile words saying, "Man, you can have it now."

Right now, my eyes are filled with tears. It hurts just to think about it. Help me, Lord. Oh, how I thank God for saving me. Glory. Hallelujah. Thank You, Jesus. This is so hard. I have to take a break and regroup myself. I'll be back in a minute… Oh, my God. Tears. Tears. Tears.

I can't help but cry and think, *I'm so grateful to be alive.*

After crying for a while – then, giving God the glory – I am back, now.

After they had used me up, they were ready to throw me away.

Is This the End?

The man that brought me there said, "Take her and do away with her. Kill her and put her body in the big dumpster in the alley."

I knew I was to die that night but someone was praying for me. God had plans for my life that I didn't know about. That's why I couldn't die there. God loved me more than the devil hated me... God won the battle over my life.

God had mercy on my soul. He saved me for such a time as this to tell what I went through forty years later. God released me to tell some of it ten years ago, in *Then and Now*, Chapter Two.

I was living in hell and running for my life. Right after I got to Michigan, I wanted to be grown and move out of Barbara's house. That was seven months after I got to the big city of Detroit. I was nineteen years old and had been in Michigan for nine months, I hadn't been there for even a year. There I was, on the floor, bleeding. I was wishing I had listened to James when he told me to go back home to Daddy and Mommy's house. My life was hanging in the balance. It is true that when you are facing death, your life does pass before you.

The Pimp

I was too far gone to change directions and go back home. I was making big money and enjoying it all. I was getting all the attention from my pimp. He was telling me and everybody else that I was *his* girl and that he loved me. I was lovin' it.

The sad part of it was I was trying to please this pimp. I saw him as the man I love and he saw me as a money maker for him. He introduced me to the bar life, to dancing, drinking, and smoking weed. I went to audition for a dancing job and got it... just like that. The devil made sure that I got it because he was trying to kill me, all the time.

Chapter 4 • Silent No More

I created exotic personas. My stage names were Brown Sugar and Chocolate Chip. I weighed only eighty nine pounds but, I had my own stage act. It would draw *crowds* of men. I began to get big – lots of money came rolling in.

Good Morning Heartache

That life began to take a toll on me. I began to drink and smoke weed. Half of the time, I was so drunk that I didn't know when or how I got home.

Many times, I thought I was going to die. It was like the devil had a contract out on me. I felt like I was in a box and couldn't get out… on a merry-go-round and couldn't get off. I was stuck in that life. That life had the best of me.

Many times, the bar got robbed. For some reason, I was always the one they would grab. They'd hold a gun to my head and tell me to get everyone's money. They could have killed me, too. Back then, if you saw a robber's face, it's goodbye for you. God had already mapped out my life. He knew it would only be a matter of time before I gave my life to Him.

I had been abused all of my childhood and teenage life. So I went for bad, trying to fight back within myself. I was still drinking, heavily.

That's when I said, "I am going to use men the way I had been used. I will get some sugar daddy to give me what I want. I'll get them to take care of me, for a while, so that I don't have to put up with any other men." I began to think that I was all of that and a bag of chips.

In the meantime, I teased death many times. As I think back, I really should not be here today… but I had a praying grandmother, a praying mother, and a praying sister. My sister's best friend was praying for me, too. They would not let it be. So, the devil didn't have a chance. The weapon was formed so many times but, it did not prosper.

> *No weapon that is formed against thee shall prosper; and every tongue that shall rise against thee in judgment thou shalt condemn. This is the heritage of the servants of the LORD, and their righteousness is of Me, saith the LORD.* (Isaiah 54:17)

Living Large and Loving It

A lot of my dancer friends ended up dead. That didn't scare me because I was ready for anybody that came my way. I was making too much money for that. I was in that lifestyle for thirteen years before God saved me. I was on the devil's roller coaster to hell. Every time I thought about leaving that life, the devil would set me up to make big… and I mean big… money. I ignored any thought of giving it all up. It was getting good and I began to like it even the more.

When you are living for the devil, doing everything he commands you to do, you don't have any fear. You don't care about anything – not even your very life. Death was at my door so many times. It did not matter if I got killed or if I did it to myself. That lifestyle had a hold on me. I thought I was at the point of no return, not knowing that God was with me all the time. You have to read the first book to get a better understanding. All of this is in it.

Chapter 4 • Silent No More

The abuse, which I was now familiar with, continued from my pimp. He was now my husband. He would beat me up and tell me that I was going to do what he said or I was not going to live. Over and over, he beat me.

One day, I went out with his mother. He didn't believe me when I told him that I had been out with his mother. He hit me so hard that my whole mouth felt like it had come apart. He had broken my jaw. I was hospitalized in Detroit's Henry Ford Hospital for six weeks. The surgeon placed four screws in my jaw to hold my mouth together. Those screws are still in my jaw, to this day. After that, he promised me that he would not hit me again. I took him back and did not press charges.

Somebody Has to Die

A few days after I got out of the hospital, the abuse began again. It went on for the next four years.

He threatened me, "If you leave me, I will find you and kill you!"

He did, in fact, try to kill me several times. I just wanted to die. So, I tried to kill myself. I took a bunch of pills. I just didn't take enough to do the job. The detail about that is available in Chapter Three of *Then and Now*.

I failed. So, he continued to torture me. One day, he shaved off all the hair on my hair so I wore wigs. We went gambling one night. He began to drink heavily. He was a mean drunk, too. He started arguing with me then slapped me so hard that my face went one way and my wig went the other. All of our friends saw my bald head. I was so embarrassed.

One night, he tied me to the bed and slowly burned me with a lit cigarette. I still have those scars on my shoulders.

I pleaded with him, "Just kill me. I don't want to live anymore." Everywhere I turned, I ended up at the devil's doorstep. The enemy was trying desperately to kill me… But God.

I started thinking, "One of us has *got* to die!" I tried to kill myself, again. But, he found me… AGAIN… and took me to the hospital. They brought me back to life…. AGAIN… But God… AGAIN.

I was so tired of fighting with him.

I figured, *Well… what do I have to lose? I will just kill him.* I did try but that didn't work. I loved that man *too* much to do anything to him… at least I thought I loved him.

It was the last thing he did to me that made me *finally* wake up. He came home one night and really tried to kill me. He put his hands around my neck and began to choke me so hard that I saw stars. I started foaming at the mouth. My eyes rolled back into my head. I was slipping out of consciousness. He almost succeeded… But God!

At that moment, I thought about all I had been through. I had made so much money. The devil made it look so easy. All the time, he wanted to take me straight to hell with him.

At that point, I thought, *Well, I'm going now*. I had felt death many times. But, *this* time it was different. So, I held my breath. I held it to make him think he had killed me.

He began yelling at me, "Bonnie, wake up. I love you. I won't do it anymore. I won't put my hands on you again. Please come back." He began to curse and swear, "What have I done? This was a good woman. This was the only woman I would ever marry. What am I going to do? What will I say?" He was just talking to himself. I wanted to hear him say, "I love you!" again and again. But, I held my breath as if I were dead. I did not move. I could have gotten an Oscar for that performance.

He left the room and went into the living room. I knew that had he known I was alive, he would have finished the job. I got up, ran to the back door, opened it, and took off running down the street, yelling, "Help me. Please, help me." I didn't have a stitch of clothes on. I realized that I had to leave him. Either he would kill me or I would kill him. I didn't want to end up in prison. So, I kept the promise I made to myself and left him... for good.

The Drug Dealer

Still dancing, I met another man at the club. He was a drug dealer that had been shot by another drug dealer and lived. Once again, I ended up with the wrong man. We became very close and started living together in a hotel.

He used drugs but never wanted *me* to do them. He habitually used drugs with the last girl he was with. That's why he got shot. So, he never wanted me to do drugs. I was fine with that because, by now, I had already had enough of alcohol, weed, drunkenness, beatings, depression, and death encounters. However, that didn't last for long.

There was a hit out on a dealer friend of his. He hadn't paid a debt for drugs he held. We didn't know anything about the hit. So, we went out to dinner with him and his girlfriend. After dinner, when we walked to the car, people were waiting outside to kill him and everyone with him.

He saw them and said, "Don't ask no questions. Get in the car."

By then, gun shots were sounding off and bullets began to hit the car. We were flying down Davidson Avenue. They were in the car behind us, continually shooting. It was like a scene in a movie. His friend's girlfriend and I were in the back seat, on the floor.

My heart was racing as I said to myself, "If *they* don't kill us, we are going to crash into another car!" But God… again. We made it to the freeway and lost them. We hid out in a filthy hotel until everything died down. Eventually, they found him and killed him and his girlfriend.

After that, I had to take a long look at my life. I began to think, *I must want to die. Every man I meet has some danger circling around him.*

First it was the drug user, then, the pimp, and then, the drug dealer. The devil had another set up for me.

My Shoes Is Hot!

While still go-go dancing, a friend, who was going to church, invited me to go with her. I had no idea that the devil would be there waiting for me… yes… in church. At church, the preacher watched me the entire service. Only a few people were there as it was not a big church. After he preached, I gave fifty dollars in the offering. That was a big offering to them, at least, back then.

Chapter 4 • Silent No More

My friend had said that he was good for predicting the lottery number. So, I put him to the test. Lo and behold, the preacher began to say, "My shoes is hot. My shoes is hot. My shoes is hot."

My friend said that they were going to play *shoes*. Of course, not being saved, I went and played the number, too. For the benefit of those who don't know anything about playing numbers, there's a Number Book. In it are code names and their corresponding numbers. For example, *shoes* might be 257, *baby* may be 764, and *stove* may be 928. Now, I don't really remember which numbers correspond with which code names. That was forty years ago. So, don't write or call me to correct me:-)

I put big money on *shoes*. Sure enough, it hit.

After church, they introduced me to the Pastor. He said, "I heard you were a go-go dancer." Immediately, lust in him began to be very obvious. He said, "I called out a number today, *shoes*. Did you get it?"

I said, "So what does all that mean?"

He replied, "Play *shoes* for three days and you will hit *big*. When you do, come see me and I will have something else for you."

So, I went to his office. He said, "You are so pretty. I couldn't keep my eyes off you in church. How long have you been dancing?"

When I told him I'd been dancing nine years, he said, "Will you dance for me? I can help you make a lot of money."

I said, "How is that?"

He said, "The Lord has given me a gift to call out numbers. If you come to church every Sunday, so that I can see you, play whatever number I call out. So, I ask again, will you dance for me?" In my mess, I began to dance for him... just to get money and a number. I made him one of my sugar daddies. By then, I had several sugar daddies taking care of me. Chapter Four of *Then and Now* gives more detail about that part of my life.

Fire, Fire, Fire

That preacher was not right. He was leading those members astray and I knew it. As long as I was making money from it, I didn't care. He began to give me money... big money. This went on for months.

One Sunday, he called out, "Fire. Fire. Fire. Fire. Fire." That meant to play *fire* and play it big.

I noticed that he was not well but I did not know he was sick. I put my money on *fire*. I played it big but, it didn't hit in three days. I didn't play it on the fourth day and it hit big.

I asked him, "Why didn't you tell me that *fire* was hitting on the fourth day.

He said, "I said *fire* five times. You should have stayed on it for five days." Thereafter, he became really sick – to the point of death.

He told me that the Lord had spoken to him, "Inform the church of what you have been doing. Ask the church for forgiveness." He and his wife stepped down from the church. He could not be a Pastor any longer.

He asked me to stay with him. I said, "For what? You are sick, don't have a church any more, can't give me any more money, and can't give me any more numbers. What would I stay for?"

He replied, "I did it for you."

I said, "Man, please. You were doing this before I met you and for how long?" I left him and never went back to that church again. My friend told me that he stayed sick for a long time and that he did eventually die.

> *For false christs and false prophets shall rise, and shall shew signs and wonders, to seduce, if it were possible, even the elect.* (Mark 13:22)

You see, the devil can throw you out a blessing that will make you think God has blessed you. All the while, it is him trying to keep you on his side. I knew that, too. The money was "good" but I was still unhappy – even with all that money.

Big Blue

I moved on to the next man – who was a police officer. By now, I was drinking really heavily, and getting drunk almost every day. The bar life had really taken a toll on me but I didn't see a way out. I wanted to talk to my mother or my sister, who was really living a saved life. However, I was too ashamed to call them.

I didn't want my mother to know that I was a go-go dancer. So, I made all of my family believe that I was the manager of the bar. One day, my brother came to the bar to see me. I told my boss that I had to act like I was the manager because I didn't want my family to know what I was really doing. I didn't want them to know… but I was making too much money to stop. I was hurting, feeling trapped and crying all the time.

I was always thinking, *One day, I'll just quit.*

You can have everything you ever thought you wanted and still be lonely, hurting. That's where I was. There was always something missing in my life. *Then*, all I thought about was big money, big lights, and big guns. I was going for bad, gambling, drinking alcohol, doing drugs, and living the "high" life. *Now*, I know it was God.

> *For what shall it profit a man, if he shall gain the whole world, and lose his own soul?* (Mark 8:36)

I met the police officer when I did a private party for some police officers. We started seeing each other. I thought I had found Mr. Right. I found out that he was married and having a baby. But… I found out too late. I had already fallen for him and he had fallen for me… at least, that's what he told me.

The affair went on for a long time. After a while, he became terribly jealous. He didn't want me to dance any more.

He said, "I don't want any other man to see your body. I don't want any other man to be looking at you… wanting to be with you."

I said, "You can't take care of me. You know it. That's how you met me, remember? Dancing." Now mind you, he's got a wife and baby.

Chapter 4 • Silent No More

He began to come to the bar. He would just sit there and watch – watch me, watch who I talked to, and see who I looked at. He got way too jealous for me. So, we began arguing and fighting. He would go to work upset. He ended up being demoted to desk duty. He couldn't drive a police car any more. He blamed me for all of this. He had his gun and I had mine. He started threatening me, telling me what he would do if I left him.

I began to complain that he could never spend the night with me. I threatened him, "One day, you're gonna call me and I'm gonna be gone." Well, he didn't believe me. I began drinking so badly and getting deeper and deeper into depression. I just wanted to die, for real. His wife found out about me and left him.

He came by the house, one night. When he got ready to leave I told him, "If you leave, I am going to shoot you." He told me to stop playing as he walked to his car. I got my gun and shot straight at him. As I was shooting, my hand went up in the air. I had been drinking a lot that day.

He jumped into the car and left. He called me and said, "You shot at me!"

I said, "I know. Next time, I won't miss."

The next day, he came by to tell me what I had done. I didn't even remember shooting at him. I was so upset at myself. I could have been in jail that day... But God. I began to cry, uncontrollably. I thought I was losing my mind. He held me and told me it would be okay.

Too Much of a Good Thing

Eventually, I decided to leave him and move on with my career as a dancer. I wanted to change my surroundings and my life, so I left town. My life only got worse. I was still drinking heavily. I was trying to drink away my problems. After I was sober, the problems and the feelings were still there. With all the money I had, you would think I would be happy. But, I wasn't; something was missing. I was always searching and crying out for something. *Now,* I know it was JESUS.

I started dancing in Canada. I made so much money until it frightened me to have so much. I remember one night, I had made so much money that I laid it on the bed and just sat there looking at it… for hours… just crying. I was unhappy, even with all the money the devil let me make. I had everything one could want. But, I was still empty.

I started dating this Hispanic man. Once again, he was a very controlling and jealous guy. An alcoholic and drug user, he was high all the time. I saw myself going right back down the same roller coaster. The devil had not gone anywhere.

He was still there, in my mind, using me, telling me all this stuff like, "You can make it big… look at where you are now."

The "Producer"

I started talking to this big movie producer who came to the bar. He wanted me to go back to California with him. He was telling me what he was going to do for me and how I was going to be making eight figures.

Chapter 4 • Silent No More

I asked him, "How much money is that?"

When he told me, I didn't believe him. He said, "This little money you are making is nothing like what you will make in Hollywood. I will be your manager. I can make it happen for you. I'll take care of everything."

Just like all the other girls, I was almost about to go. However, I felt something in me say, "No. Don't do that. You will never come back. You think you've been used. When *he* gets through with you, it will be no more *you*." So, I told him, "I don't think I will do that just yet. I will give you an answer when you come back to Michigan next month."

Thank God that I listened to the voice in my heart. I found out that he was part of a sex slave ring. He would take the girls he recruited, put them in a house and sell them to men who visited these sex slave houses. He would get the girls hooked on drugs so that they wouldn't know or feel anything.

All glory be to God… I got saved that next month. I thought about what could have been… even after I got saved. I now belonged to God. The devil had to loose me and let me go. The devil didn't want me to live. He wanted to take me straight to hell with him. I was on my way… But God.

My home in Canada was a hotel room where I lived for the next four months. I would come back home on the weekends to the home I had bought with the money I made dancing.

5
Don't Go Back

Emma and her best friend lived in North Carolina. My mother lived in Beatrice, Alabama. They continued to pray for me, holding me up before the Lord, asking Him to save me. I was in my mess. Don't give up on your loved ones. Continue to pray. Watch God bring them in. It's just a matter of time. My sister knew what I was doing – dancing, drinking, and living the bar life on my way to hell. But, my mother didn't know.

> *Confess your faults one to another, and pray one for another, that ye may be healed. The effectual fervent prayer of a righteous man availeth much.* (James 5:16)

Emma just wouldn't give up on me. She was always calling me. I didn't answer the phone sometimes because I knew what she was going to say.

It was never, "Hey girl. We miss you. How much money did you make today? What about all those trips you are going on? How you doing?" It was always, "Hey. I am just calling to tell you what God showed me in the spirit concerning you."

I would reply, "Okay. What did you see *this* time? Did I hit the lotto real big? Did you see me rich with a big house on a hill? Ha. Ha. Ha." I would laugh.

Then and Now, Part II

Oh, she did not like it when I would say that! She said, "I dreamed that you were giving your life to the Lord."

I would really laugh, "Me? Oh no… not me." Half of the time, I was drunk when I talked to her.

I always wanted to talk to her, though. Growing up, Emma and I were very close – and, we still are. I just didn't want to hear all of the other mess about GOD all the time. We almost never talked about the family because she was always telling me all the things I didn't want to hear.

She continued to say stuff like, "What you are doing is not worth it. You are going to die out there." At the end, before she hung up, she would say, "I love you and want the best for you. I will talk to you later." I was glad every time she hung up. I thank God for her, every day, for not giving up on me.

Late one Friday night, I was getting ready to go back to Niagara Falls, Canada, to dance in a huge production. This was a big one. The phone rang. It was Emma. God had definitely given her something about me this time.

Countless times, she has called to tell me that she saw me dead. She would always warn me to stop and give my life to the Lord. I didn't want to hear that. I was making all that money. I didn't have to give anyone any of it.

I would say, "How am I supposed to make it? You know how much money I make?"

So, she stopped calling saying, "Every time God showed me something about you, I have called and told you. But, you gave it no mind."

Chapter 5 • Don't Go Back

Tag...Toe

Emma said, "God said, don't go back to Canada anymore!"

I said, "What? I never told you that I was in Canada."

She said, "I know… but God did." That was the first thing that messed me up. She knew I was working in Canada though I never told her. No one in my family knew that. She said, "You won't make it back. I saw you with a tag on your big toe. We had to come and identify your body. It had been in the mud for weeks."

I replied, "I ain't going to Canada." I knew, all the while, that I was on my way the very next morning. She said, "I don't care what you say. I know what God showed me. I saw you with a tag on your big toe, Bonnie. This thing has troubled my spirit. I've been up praying and coming against the devil on your behalf. I've been declaring that 'this soul, devil, you will not have. She belongs to God. Step back, devil. Loose her mind, her body, and her soul and let her go. Satan, I bind you on every side. The blood of Jesus is against you. This is God's property.'"

I said to myself, *Here we go again. She is going to pray and pray and pray. I've got to get some sleep.* I didn't want to hear that right then. I began to play with her like I always did, "I am going to play *big toe* and *tag* in the lotto tomorrow. When I hit it, I am going to send you some money."

She never wanted any of my dirty money. She never wanted to hear me say I was going to play what God had given her to tell me. She truly is a great, anointed woman of God. Everything she told me that God gave her was always on time

– everything… every time. I began to get a bad feeling about going back to Canada.

She said, "I have given you what God gave me. Now, it is up to you to open up your ears and hear what God is saying to you this time."

He is Calling

After she said all that about seeing me with a tag on my big toe, who wants to hear anything else she would have to say? Not me, for real. She got on my *last* nerve… and I mean my last. After that call, I had made up my mind not to talk to her for a while… a long while.

I am so tired of her with all this stuff. Why doesn't she just leave me alone? I don't want to be saved. Those were the thoughts that were racing through my mind. I wanted to just go away somewhere… away from it all.

Something began to happen to me. God began to deal with me that night. The moment for me to give my life to the Lord was drawing close.

I did not know it but God had another plan for my life. I went to hell and back to tell my testimony, "Jesus saves and will save you if you let Him. He is calling you… even in your running. It is over. You've got to say, 'YES,' just like I did." The money was good. However, to tell you the truth; I was really tired of that kind of living.

My sister had called me many times… and I mean many… and said these kinds of things to me. But, *that* night it was different.

Chapter 5 • Don't Go Back

I began to lay there and cry, "Why did she call me? Why couldn't she have waited until I got back on Monday?" I began to feel the tag on my toe. I got worried. Her call shook me up that night.

All I could hear was, "Don't go back to Canada. We had to come and identify your body." It was like she left her voice in my head. I couldn't sleep. I cried the rest of the night.

When morning came, I hadn't gotten much sleep. I called my girlfriend and said, "Like I always say, 'It's time to go make that money.' I will be there in a little while." The weather was awful; it was snowing and the road was very slippery.

I kept hearing in my spirit, "Don't go back to Canada… tags… big toe."

I began to yell, "Emma, get out of my mind. I will be alright." My heart got so heavy that I could hardly drive… I was fighting to hold back the tears.

By now, the snow had really begun to fall so I lost control of the car. My car began to skid from the fast lane… to the middle lane… to the slow lane… to completely off the road. The car was inches from running into an icy river. As the car began to slide through all that traffic I could see hell. Hell was very dark, extremely black.

As we slid down the hill, I cried out, "We are going to die. They will be coming to identify me with a tag on my big toe! Emma was right."

My girlfriend cried out, "NO! NO! NO!" She was screaming so loud in my ear that I completely lost control of my car – which was a brand new Lincoln Town Car. I closed my eyes and began to give up. Then, I saw this bright, bright, bright light and fire. It was bright yet dark at the same time.

I grabbed her by the collar and screamed, "We are going to die. Do you hear me?" As fear gripped my heart, all I could hear was, "Don't go back to Canada. We are coming to identify your body with a tag on your big toe." The devil tried to take me out three times that night.

Just Jump

After I finally reached the hotel in Canada, I got very drunk, trying to forget about what I'd just gone through.

The next day, lying down in the hotel room, the devil began to talk, "Just go to the window and jump out. No one will find you because no one cares about you."

I got up crying and went to the window. The room was on a high floor. I looked all around; tears were rolling down my face. I almost yielded to what the devil was saying. However, when I put one leg up on the window sill; I fell back onto the floor. I tried to get up and I couldn't. I lay there, for hours, until my next show. I was just sobbing.

Still on the roller coaster, the devil had turned me into an alcoholic. I got so drunk after that.

I thought, *I am trying to die and can't. Why can't I?* God had my life already planned out. I didn't know it then. During that period, Emma and others were on a fast, interceding for me.

Chapter 5 ● Don't Go Back

I called Emma when I got back to the hotel. I could hear her weeping on the other end of the phone. "I fasted and prayed the whole week on your behalf. I lay before the Lord that He would cover you with His blood. I prayed that He wouldn't let you die in your sin. He has told me that He would save you. I believe it."

After hanging up, I cried for a while because my sister was hurt. It hurt me, too. You see, I still had a heart. I just didn't want to be saved. She still didn't give up on me. She continued to lay before the Lord on my behalf. I believe, at that point, she was getting tired of going back and forth with me about my salvation. Nevertheless, God kept her praying until I gave up and said, "Yes!" to Him. She kept on praying and fasting until she birthed me into the kingdom. Thank You, JESUS! I talked about my dramatic conversion in Chapter Six of *Then and Now*.

Then and Now, Part II

THEN – Bonnie Baker: Wednesday, July 2, 1975. Detroit, Michigan.

Chapter 5 • Don't Go Back

NOW – Bonnie Baker: Monday, September 2, 2013. Detroit, Michigan.

6

A Call From God

After much, much prayer by others, the Lord Jesus Christ saved me in 1982. I've been living for Him over thirty years. I have been at the International Gospel Center (IGC) all that time. This was the place to be. Here, God is moving, saving, delivering, and setting people free.

IGC is where I met my husband, Dean. We got married nine months after I got there. We've been married 30 years and counting. We have four daughters, Tawana, Kenyatta, Chantel, and LaChisa; one grandson, little Ivan; and there are nine babies in Heaven – three boys and six girls.

Saturday, September 10, 1983 – Dean and Bonnie on their wedding day. Ecorse, Michigan.

My husband and I began to seek the Lord. For the next five years of our marriage, we would be put to the test. During that five year span, at one point or another, we had no money and no jobs. We lost a home.

We lived in a roach infested apartment. We turned the lights out to go to bed. In the morning, the kitchen counter was teeming with roaches. At work one day, I opened my purse and out jumped a bunch of roaches. My husband had to replace the muffler on every car we had so they wouldn't make so much noise. It was hard but we keep on seeking the Lord with prayer and fasting. We just took it one day at a time.

The Saints

The Lord gave me much favor with the saints in the church. One who had a profound effect on our lives was Mother Poole. Mother Poole witnessed everywhere we went. She always prayed for people she came in contact with. Mother Poole taught me how to wait on the Lord. She blessed us and was always there for us. She kept us in church because we were her ride to church. She was such an anointed vessel of God. Being around such a holy woman of God made us seek the Lord like never before. We kept a fasted and prayer-filled life.

Mother Poole would always say, "The Lord is going to bless you and give you back everything you lost." I thank God for putting her in our lives.

My friend, Marlene, and her husband lived across the street from us. They were also members of IGC. They were a blessing to us too many times to mention. They prayed for us. They believed God with us that He would bring us out. They fed us, gave us money, gave us clothes, and helped us so much more. They are true friends, even to this day.

My friend, Gloria, is from Mobile, Alabama. Just like me, she's from down south. Our hometowns aren't very far apart. She prayed and walked us through a lot of suffering until God blessed us. She gave me clothes to wear and food to eat.

Chapter 6 • A Call From God

My sister, Pastor Hopkins and her late husband, Pastor Lonnie White, prayed until God was formed in us. They prayed until we had the keeping power to stay saved and trust God... no matter what. They also walked us though many things.

Fasting and Prayer

As we began to seek the Lord, two of our friends, my brother and my sister-in-law went on a forty day fast having nothing but water. On the twenty-sixth day, we came off of the fast because one of the women on the fast became ill. We later found out that she was pregnant.

Monday, September 2, 2013 – The Baker Family poses for a family portrait in their residence in Michigan. Front row left to right: Chantel, Bonnie, Ivan (6 months old) and LaChisa. Standing left to right: Kenyatta, Dean and Tawana.

Then and Now, Part II

I wanted to have a baby so that we could become a family. But, it didn't happen when I wanted it to. By faith, I would wear maternity dresses to become pregnant and it still didn't happen. After the twenty-sixth day, I got pregnant. My sister-in-law got pregnant, too. Our children are seven months apart.

During my pregnancy, we were still going through hardships. Our gas got cut off right after I got pregnant. It stayed off throughout my pregnancy. My sister-in-law, Ora, gave us a hot plate. In the winter months, Dean would warm me up water on it so that I could take a warm bath. He would just take cold baths. No sooner than we could get all the water warmed, the water would be cold again. We still have the hot plate to this day.

Same Ride...Different Riders

Once I was saved and had children, the devil knew his time was up with me. So, he tried to take my children on the same roller coaster. My daughter, Kenyatta, loved the "Barney Show." When she was three, we had to sing the Barney song every day and every night.

> *I love you, you love me. We're a happy family. With a great big hug and a kiss from me to you. Won't you say you love me too?*

At age six, the "Barney Show" came to nearby Northland Mall. Kenyatta was chosen to talk about "Barney". The local news-crew came to our house the next day to interview her. The following day, an article about it was in the newspaper. The "Barney Show" wanted her to appear on the show. Since it was out of town and she was only in first grade, we didn't want her to go. It was going to pay well... But God. I saw the devil at work, trying to take our daughter down the same road he had taken me on.

At six and seven, Chantel and LaChisa auditioned for the play "The Wizard of Oz" in Detroit. They beat out six hundred children and got to play Munchkins. Backstage, we met the other actors. Sure enough, the same thing happened to them that happened to Kenyatta. The show wanted them to go on the road. Again, it would have paid some good money. Besides, they were only six and seven years old. We didn't want to take them out of school.

The devil was trying so hard to get our minds on him. He tried to set the same trap for my girls that he caught me in... But God.

> *Pull me out of the net that they have laid privily for me: for thou art my strength.* (Psalm 31:4)

> *He must also have a good reputation with outsiders, so that he will not fall into disgrace and into the devil's trap.* (1 Timothy 3:7 NIV)

Despise Not Small Beginnings

We kept God first and did not accept anything the devil had to offer. We began to go through hardships – financially and every other way. It is funny how the devil can bring thoughts back to your mind. I began to think back on how much money we could have made if we had let the girls do the shows... But God.

> *But my God shall supply all your need according to his riches in glory by Christ Jesus.* (Philippians 4:19)

God told me to...

> *Trust in the* LORD *with all your heart and lean not on your own understanding; in all your ways submit to him, and he will make your paths straight.* (Proverbs 3:5-6 NIV)

You see, God had my back.

> *I will instruct you and teach you in the way you should go; I will counsel you with my loving eye on you.* (Psalm 32:8 NIV)

I was bought with a price. I had lived for the devil too long. Now, I belong to God. I was tired of the devil.

The Overflow

After waiting on God for ten years – and not selling out to the devil – God began to bless us. In 1993, our breakthrough came. We began to walk in our blessing. It's been a road of blessing. Don't sell out to the devil. You *can* make it.

> *Wait on the Lord: be of good courage, and He shall strengthen thine heart: wait, I say, on the Lord.* (Psalm 27:14)

> *Wait on the* LORD, *and keep his way, and he shall exalt thee to inherit the land: when the wicked are cut off, thou shalt see it.* (Psalm 37:34)

> *But they that wait upon the* LORD *shall renew their strength; they shall mount up with wings as eagles; they shall run, and not be weary; and they shall walk and not faint.* (Isaiah 40:31)

We were living in the city. I was very comfortable there but God had other plans for us. We moved to the suburbs… into the house God had for us. The Lord began to bless us real good. We began to walk in the overflow from the seeds we had planted.

Chapter 6 • A Call From God

> *I planted the seed, Apollos watered it, but God has been making it grow. So neither the one who plants nor the one who waters is anything, but only God, who makes things grow. The one who plants and the one who waters have one purpose, and they will each be rewarded according to their own labor.* (1 Corinthians 3:6-8 NIV)

For you that are going through hardships, wait upon the Lord.

> *For His anger endureth but a moment; in His favour is life: weeping may endure for a night, but joy cometh in the morning.* (Psalm 30:5)

We were walking in our blessing. You can read all about it on page 63 of *Then and Now*.

7
Visions and Dreams

Throughout these thirty one years of salvation, God has given me many visions, dreams, and messages.

> *And it shall come to pass afterward, that I will pour out my spirit upon all flesh; and your sons and your daughters shall prophesy, your old men shall dream dreams, your young men shall see visions.* (Joel 2:28)

I remember the time that God took me to hell. He walked with me and showed me many things. I saw the devil. The look that he gave me frightened me so badly that I was ready to go. Jesus said, "You must walk through this. I must show you this." I saw many people who I knew: many saints, family, and some close friends. I cried bitter tears until my face was beet red.

When we passed back by the devil, he was laughing and pointing at me – I held on to Jesus as tight as I could. It was so hot until the walls were melting. Fire was coming out from people's eyes, ears, mouths, and noses. Their entire bodies were on fire. You could hear their cries and mourning as they burned. That was the worst thing I'd ever seen. I don't ever want to see that again. I don't even want to think that some of my family and friends are there. It was so bad, I couldn't take it.

Then Jesus said, "Tell them to turn from their sin. Tell them what you saw. Tell them I am coming soon. If My people, who are called by My name, shall humble themselves, and pray, and seek My face, and turn from their wicked ways; then, will I hear from heaven, and will forgive their sin, and will heal their land" (2 Chronicles 7:14).

I Went to Heaven

In another vision the Lord gave me, I went to Heaven. Now, *this* vision I liked. I didn't want to come back to earth. I began to walk down this gold road. I ended up in a garden where everyone was congregated. It was so beautiful. Everything was white. There were so many flowers. The flowers were always in bloom.

I began to walk around. I came upon a long line of people. I asked them what they were waiting in line for. No one said a word. As far as I could see, people were shaking hands; all the way down the line. It was the receiving line to welcome saints into Heaven. I got in the line. Behold, there was everyone I knew. They didn't say anything to me or I to them. But, we knew each other.

All the saints that went home to be with the Lord before the last day were in that line. So, I knew I would see my Dad and Mom.

I began to ask, "Where is my Daddy and Mommy?"

Someone said, "Come down here." I went down a little ways and there was my Daddy and Mommy.

Chapter 7 • Visions and Dreams

I began to cry out with a loud voice, "Mom, Dad, I'm here. I made it. I miss you all so much. I love you!" They both smiled. I was so happy to see them.

I said, "Where are my babies?" There they were. Each one cried, "Mommy. Mommy. Mommy. Mommy. Mommy. Mommy. Mommy. Mommy. Mommy." All nine of them said it. I fell down and cried, "Here I am!" I felt myself hugging them, kissing them, and saying, "I am right here." I wanted them to see their Daddy. I didn't know where he was. But I knew he was there.

I began to see all the men in the Bible we read about. Moses had long, long hair hanging down his back. His face was as bright as light. There was one thing I didn't understand. I began to cry very hard about it. I didn't see my husband and my other children.

I said, "Where is Jesus? Jesus! Jesus! Where is He?" I felt someone touch my shoulder. I looked and it was Jesus.

Crying, I bowed down and worshiped Him, "Jesus, thank You for dying for me and giving me salvation."

When I looked up to see His face, He turned and said, "It's time to go back to your husband and children." The next thing I knew, I was back, lying in my bed and out of the vision.

Overtake...Overcome

In another dream, the Lord gave me it was very dark. I began to look up to Heaven. I saw a plane as it traveled along. I watched as it began to turn into a white horse. The horse was flying, just like the plane.

Then, the Lord began to speak to me, "My people have to conquer and go forth to overtake, to overcome, to have authority over the devil." Many souls were riding on this white horse. Saints that had made it in were given a crown.

> *And I saw, and behold a white horse: and he that sat on him had a bow; and a crown was given unto him: and he went forth conquering, and to conquer.* (Revelations 6:2)

8

The Four Seasons

In another vision, I saw a gigantic – and I mean HUGE – clock. It read 11:57 PM: Three minutes to 12:00 AM. The clock was so big until I got lost looking at it. Then God said, "Tell My people that 'Time is winding up.' I am coming back to take My people home." God's timing is everything.

> To every thing there is a season, and a time to every purpose under the heaven: A time to be born, and a time to die; a time to plant, and a time to pluck up that which is planted; A time to kill, and a time to heal; a time to break down, and a time to build up; A time to weep, and a time to laugh; a time to mourn, and a time to dance; A time to cast away stones, and a time to gather stones together; a time to embrace, and a time to refrain from embracing; A time to get, and a time to lose; a time to keep, and a time to cast away; A time to rend, and a time to sew; a time to keep silence, and a time to speak; A time to love, and a time to hate; a time of war, and a time of peace. (Ecclesiastes 3:1-8)

God's timing is perfect, never early, never late. So, why is it so hard to believe? It's hard to wait for God to answer every prayer in our timing. How long we have to wait is based on God's timing and how well we go through while we're waiting.

Let's look at the children of Israel. They grumbled, complained, and whined the entire time they were in the desert. It should have taken a lot less than 40 years to make the eleven day journey through the wilderness. What's even worse, only two of the original two million people actually made it in to the promised land. Why? They were the only ones who had the right attitude.

Your Attitude Determines Your Altitude

Our attitude can keep us from God's best. Our blessing can be held up for some time. It makes you wonder: how many things have we missed because of all the grumbling, complaining, and whining when God's timing didn't line up with our own. What we missed was God's best.

Some people plan a whole bunch of stuff and expect God to bless it. God expects you to pray first and *then* plan. It took me a long time to get to this point in my life. Only move forward with your plan *if* you've asked God first and you know that it is the will of God. Get a witness and a confirmation. If you're doing what God tells you to do, then, His favor and anointing will be on it. It has to work because it is God.

Just because something doesn't work, doesn't mean God isn't in it. He may have a better option, a better deal, or better arrangements. His timing means exactly that. If you trust Him then there is no reason to be discouraged. That is what we have to do as we wait for God to come through for us. It is hard to trust when you can't see it. Don't get discouraged and give up. Isn't it worth waiting on God's timing?

Gods timing is throughout the Bible.

> *And Abraham took the wood of the burnt offering, and laid it upon Isaac his son; and he took the fire in his hand, and a knife;*

Chapter 8 • The Four Seasons

and they went both of them together. And Isaac spake unto Abraham his father, and said, My father: and he said, Here am I, my son. And he said, Behold the fire and the wood: but where is the lamb for a burnt offering? And Abraham said, My son, God will provide himself a lamb for a burnt offering: so they went both of them together. And they came to the place which God had told him of; and Abraham built an altar there, and laid the wood in order, and bound Isaac his son, and laid him on the altar upon the wood. And Abraham stretched forth his hand, and took the knife to slay his son. And the angel of the LORD called unto him out of heaven, and said, Abraham, Abraham: and he said, Here am I. And he said, Lay not thine hand upon the lad, neither do thou any thing unto him: for now I know that thou fearest God, seeing thou hast not withheld thy son, thine only son from me. (Genesis 22:6-12)

There it is, in verse 13… God's timing.

And Abraham lifted up his eyes, and looked, and behold behind him a ram caught in a thicket by his horns: and Abraham went and took the ram, and offered him up for a burnt offering in the stead of his son. (Genesis 22:13)

Later in that chapter, God said:

That in blessing I will bless thee, and in multiplying I will multiply thy seed as the stars of the heaven, and as the sand which is upon the sea shore; and thy seed shall possess the gate of his enemies. (Genesis 22-17)

Joseph was sent to Egypt. A series of events led to the rescue of his family. He was a dreamer. His own brothers cast him into a pit to kill him. All of it was in God's timing; it was the will of God. The devil meant it for evil. God worked it out for his good. Over all of Egypt, Joseph was second in command, second only to Pharaoh.

There are many other stories in the Bible about God's timing. He worked things out for His people. In the New Testament, Acts 9:1-29, a man named Ananias saw a vision to go to Straight Street and preach to a man named Saul. He wasn't very eager to do this because Saul persecuted the church. Saul had his own encounter with Jesus on the road to Damascus.

> *And as he journeyed, he came near Damascus: and suddenly, there shined round about him a light from heaven: And he fell to the earth, and heard a voice saying unto him, 'Saul, Saul, why persecutest thou Me'? And he said, 'Who art thou, Lord'? And the Lord said, I am Jesus Whom thou persecutest: it is hard for thee to kick against the pricks. And he, trembling and astonished said, Lord, what wilt thou have Me to do? And the Lord said unto him, Arise, and go into the city, and it shall be told thee what thou must do.* (Acts 9:3-6)

After all of that, he was ready to hear God. He was ready to receive the message. He was a chosen vessel unto God. Saul increased more in strength – in God's timing. Look at all that Saul had to go through. Sometimes, it is just best to obey God from the beginning. Saul is the same man who we know later as Paul.

God sent Jesus according to His perfect time...not too early... not too late. He came – at just the right time – to save this world. I am glad that Jesus came when He did. I am glad He saved my soul. I am glad that He forgave my sin. I am glad that He is a loving God. I am glad that He went to the cross. I am glad that after three days, He rose again. I am glad that He lives forever. I am glad that He sits on the right side of His Father and prays for us continually. I

Chapter 8 • The Four Seasons

am glad that when the time was fully come, God sent His Son, Jesus.

> *But when the fullness of the time was come, God sent forth his Son, made of a woman, made under the law.* (Galatians 4:4)

Buy Back Some Time

The Bible says that you can "redeem the time" (Ephesians 5:16). To redeem means to recover, repay, repurchase. God will let you buy back some time. As God said through the prophet Joel, "I will restore to you the years the locusts have eaten" (Joel 2:25).

So, if you have blown your opportunities and missed your time of recovery or success, you can repent and buy back some time from God. God will put you back in the race and rewind the clock. He will let you start over again. You can start from where you were before. You will probably have to go through, time and time again. God has to mold you and make you into what He would have you to be. He loves us just that much. But, it's all in His timing. I had to wait for my time to come… for God to save me… after much prayer.

What Season Are You In?

God has made it easy for us to understand and discover His timing. He made it simple by giving us the seasons in life. You must understand that everything has a season.

> *To every thing there is a season, and a time to every purpose under the heaven.* (Ecclesiastes 3:1)

To know the time for everything, you need to understand that every activity has a season. Seasons are God's clue to timing. God's timing in your life can be discerned by determining what season you're in. When you find out the season you're in, you can act accordingly.

To find out God's time, you simply need to ask yourself, "What season am I in?"

You may be in a time in your life when everything seems dead and lifeless – just like winter. It may seem dead but, this is a time for you to dream and dream big. This is not wasted time. It seems nicer to live in a warm climate where there are no seasons. In a paradise like that, however, there is no opportunity to dream and plan.

In this life, God meant for us to experience all four seasons. Yes. Winter seems to be the dreariest. Oh, how it is needed, though.

Just as there are four seasons of nature, there are four seasons of life. Each season responds to a particular action that you need to take. For example, there is a time to plant and a time to reap. How do you know when it's time to reap? You know it's time when the harvest is ripe. We also have to go through the four seasons of life. They are: winter, spring, summer, and fall. Each of these seasons demands a particular action on our part.

During winter, you need to dream and plan. In spring, you need to plant and grow. In summer, you must water and prepare. During fall, you finally reap and distribute. What season are you in now?

Chapter 8 • The Four Seasons

Are you in your winter season? It is time to go through, dream and plan.

You may say, "I've been going through. It looks like everything is going wrong?"

Are you in your spring season? It is time to plant.

Say, "I am going to plant correctly this time. When it grows up, it will be right."

Are you in your summer season? It is time to water and keep silent.

Say, "I've got to keep watering by fasting, praying, and reading the Word of God. I'll let my words be few and seasoned with grace. I am going to keep what I got this time."

Are you in your fall season? Reap and be blessed.

Say, "I'm finally coming out. It's my time and my season to be blessed. I dreamed and planned. I planted and watched it grow. I watered it by keeping silent. Now, it's time for me to reap. It's time for me to speak. It's time for me to get… not to lose anymore. It's time for me to be healed. It's time for me to be built up. It's time for me to receive."

He's Got the Whole World in His Hands

Remember Ecclesiastes 3:1, "To every thing there is a season, and a time to every purpose under the heaven." Remember that what God has for you is for you. But… it's all in His timing.

God does not work on *our* time.

> *But, beloved, be not ignorant of this one thing, that one day is with the Lord as a thousand years, and a thousand years as one day.* (2 Peter 3:8)

Just think. There are 24 hours in a day. One second could be five to ten years to God. But, to us it doesn't look like it's *ever* going to end. You may be saying, "Lord, when will I come out? How long, Lord? I've been in this trial too long."

You call on mercy. You are calling for grace. You are begging God to help you. You are giving up to the Lord. Still… nothing is happening. It looks like it's getting worse and worse, by the day. Just wait on the Lord. I have learned to stay there and wait on God until it's time to come out. It all depends on God's timing. It's all in His hands.

> *Now unto him that is able to do exceeding abundantly above all that we ask or think, according to the power that worketh in us.* (Ephesians 3:20)

God is certainly great and worthy of glory and our praise. Our prayers don't always get answered the way we hope. Nevertheless, it would blow our minds if the Lord showed us even a glimpse of what He does for us when we pray.

You are pleading with God, "I can't hear you, Lord. I've been praying. I've repented of my sins." You've got faith but nothing has been happening. Yes. It can be very frustrating.

The timing of God is everything. If God gave us everything we want, He knows that we would forget about Him for a while. We would stop praying, stop fasting, and stop seeking Him. We'd go into our comfort zones. Remember, His timing is everything. It might not come when we want it but He is always on time.

Chapter 8 • The Four Seasons

Everything that looks good ain't always good. Making the wrong decision will cost you. You *will* go through. Can you think of something you did or said that, at the time, seemed like it was from God? You regretted it afterwards. Personally, I can think of *many* things.

You will not come out until God says, "It's time." Trusting in God's timing and having peace with it is the key.

There is a time for coming out and a time for going through. When I look back over my life, I've been up and I've been down. In spite of my situation, in spite of my circumstance, in spite of what I am going through right now, I see how far God has brought me. I can't help but praise Him. I can't help but thank the Lord. I can't help but trust Him. I can't do anything *but* trust Him.

Hope Deferred

Back then, I wanted to be a movie actor. I almost made it. But, God had other plans for my life at that time. My dream came true, thirty four years later.

One night, I was online, looking for someone to turn *Then and Now* into a movie. I found a production company and called it the next morning. Shortly after that, I got called in for an audition. The audition went well and I won the role as a lawyer in a movie entitled, *The Invisible*. In one scene, I was driving my car. Other characters were also driving cars. Homeless people attacked us in our cars.

It was very exciting to work as an actor and be a part of a movie. I enjoyed it to the fullest. I got a chance to talk with the producer and director. I gave them each a copy of *Then and Now*. Since then, I have received many calls to audition. *The Invisible* is a great movie. It will be coming out soon.

No one knew about this except my family. It isn't good to tell everything too soon. Sometimes, you need to wait until God brings it to pass.

9
Wake Up and Call on Jesus

God began to speak to me, "Wake up and call on Me." He wanted me to warn His people. So, I began to preach that message, "Wake up and call on Jesus."

And that, knowing the time, that now it is high time to awake out of sleep: for now is our salvation nearer than when we believed. (Roman 13:11)

1 Corinthians 11:30 says, "For this cause many are weak and sickly among you, and many sleep." God is saying that many of His people are asleep in the spirit. But, it's time to awake and be about your Father's business. Time is winding up. Be ready and not getting ready.

For yourselves know perfectly that the day of the Lord so cometh as a thief in the night. (1 Thessalonians 5:2)

Let us wake up from our slumber. Call on Jesus while it is still day.

Let's not be like those who call on Jesus only when they need Him and then, say, "I'll see You when I need You again." Those people fall right back to sleep, in the spirit, and into sin.

Wherefore he saith, Awake thou that sleepest, and arise from the dead, and Christ shall give thee light. (Ephesians 5:14)

Then and Now, Part II

These are some things that can keep you asleep:
1. Regression
2. Suppression
3. Depression
4. Oppression
5. Obsession
6. Possession

Therefore let us not sleep, as do others; but let us watch and be sober. (1 Thessalonians 5:6)

Messages from the Lord

Here are some messages the Lord gave me which were a blessing to the people of God. They are still available to anyone who wants to hear them:

Wait on Me
I Don't Want to Be in Sodom
Effected Change
If It Ain't One Thing, It's Another
You Are Coming Out
It's Your Time to be Blessed
It's Time
Time Out, Cry Out
Stand Up
Virtuous Woman
God Is Calling You
Broken Piece Don't Mean Broken Promise
Stay Focused. Doubt Not
Keep Your Eyes on Jesus

Push Again and Pray Again
Thank God for the Overflow
The Seeds that You Plant
Through Prayer I Made It (James 5:16)
Walking in the Obedience of God
Take It Back
The Big Tree
You've Got Power So Let's Use It
Nothing Shall Be Impossible
In Seven Days
If You Believe
Coming Out of your Trial
Don't Sell Out before It's Over
What Do You See?

Chapter 9 • Wake Up and Call on Jesus

I Am that I Am	Do You Know Your Call in God
God Heard Your Prayer	Can These Bones Live
Don't Be Ashamed of Your Past	Lord Breathe on Me
One Man Can Make a Difference (Roman 5:19)	What Do You Expect?
	Stand Up and Live
God's Timing	Don't Give Up
He Will	God Will Deliver
Growing in God	Keep Your Eyes on Jesus
Push One More Push	God Deliver Me from the Fire
It's Time to Deliver	Fill Me the More Lord
Catch the Devil and Don't Let Him Go	Another Level
	Call to Action
It's Time to Recover It All	My Change
Another Touch	Let Nothing Separate You from God
Devil Let It Go	

Shout, for God Has Given It to You

You don't have to wait until the battle is over. You can do what we did, SHOUT.

> And it shall come to pass, that when they make a long blast with the ram's horn, and when ye hear the sound of the trumpet, all the people shall shout with a great shout; and the wall of the city shall fall down flat, and the people shall ascend up every man straight before him. And Joshua had commanded the people, saying, Ye shall not shout, nor make any noise with your voice, neither shall any word proceed out of your mouth, until the day I bid you shout; then shall ye shout. And it came to pass at the seventh time, when the priests blew with the trumpets, Joshua said unto the people, Shout; for the LORD hath given you the city. (Joshua 6:5,10,16)

God gave us the power to hang in there when things get rough. He let me know that *we* have the power. When the enemy comes in like a flood, we just need to use that power against him.

> *But ye shall receive power, after that the Holy Ghost is come upon you: and ye shall be witnesses unto me both in Jerusalem, and in all Judaea, and in Samaria, and unto the uttermost part of the earth.* (Act 1:8)

As people of God, we have that power to use. However, a lot of times, we fall right back into the devil's hands. We let him catch us with our guards down. If you are weak and going through, remember that you've got power.

> *They shall take up serpents; and if they drink any deadly thing, it shall not hurt them; they shall lay hands on the sick, and they shall recover.* (Mark 16:18)

When you realize who you are in Christ, receiving from Him becomes so much easier. You've got the power to loose your finances, your job, your surroundings, your children, your house, your husband, your wife, your mind, your body, and your soul. You've got the power to loose everything that the devil is holding up.

I am glad the Lord saved me when He did. If the Lord had not saved me, I would be dead. I know that. That's why I praise Him like I do. You don't know like I know where He brought me from. I went from a hell-bound existence to life in Christ. I am living to live again. I am living to see all my babies and all my loved ones again. I want to see Jesus again. I love Him with all my heart, mind and soul.

Chapter 9 • Wake Up and Call on Jesus

The Prequel

If you have not read *Then and Now*, it is a must read. You really need to have read it to get the most from this book. You can read about my husband. He's the blessing God was holding for me until I got saved. He was mine before the foundation of the world. He was mine, even when I was in my mother's womb. He was mine before I said my first word. That's why I couldn't die. GOD had him waiting on me and me waiting on him.

I couldn't die because God had a plan for my life. Dean, the girls, and little Ivan were in it. I love our little grandson. Two months after he was born, he was hospitalized for ten days. He had bronchitis and several other conditions. He was released from the hospital and one month later had to go right back. The devil still tried... even with our grandson... A lot of prayer went up for him. Now, he is fine and getting fatter by the day.

I was in the 11th grade when I got married the first time. I didn't finish the 12th grade with my class. I never really liked school... when I went. However, I always wanted to go to college. So, I took a placement test to determine whether or not I could be admitted to college. My score was high enough to start. So, in 2011, I enrolled in college. I have been on the Dean's List for four semesters in a row with a 3.8 to 4.0 grade point average. Soon, I will have my bachelor's degree. This is a great accomplishment for me... at my age... after all I've been through... I am so proud of myself.

I thank God for all the love, support, and understanding I've received from readers. God let me know that this book would be a blessing to the body of Christ, as well as, everyone who reads it. Everything we go through in our lives can be used for His glory. I never would have guessed that my life would end up in a book. I couldn't have imagined the number of people who would read it and get set free from everything the devil could serve up: alcohol, drugs, gambling, abuse, imprisonment, depression, even, encounters with death.

I belong to God. I have been bought with a price by Jesus. *Now*, I live for Him. I went through all that for such a time as this.

> *And he said unto them, I must preach the kingdom of God to other cities also: for therefore am I sent.* (Luke 4:43)
>
> *Cry aloud, spare not, lift up thy voice like a trumpet, and shew My people their transgression, and the house of Jacob their sins.* (Isaiah 58:1)
>
> *Then the master told his servant, 'Go out to the roads and country lanes and compel them to come in, so that my house will be full.* (Luke 14:23 NIV)

Look for my upcoming book, *Coming Out of Your Pain*. It's really going to be powerful. As you can see, I do enjoy writing. But, as I sit here finishing up my third book, it's bittersweet. It's saddens me that my mom and dad are not here to see how the Lord has blessed their baby girl. Oh, how they would be rejoicing.

As my baby brother, Nate, used to say, "Go, Dinxie Gal!"

The familiar scripture, John 3:16 says, "For God so loved the world, that He gave His only begotten Son, that whosoever believeth in Him should not perish, but, have everlasting life." That's the life I'm living for – eternal life.

10
My Family and their Words

My wife, Bonnie, is my life, my love, and my best friend. I want to begin by saying, "I thank God for you. I thank Him for giving me you."

For this cause shall a man leave his father and mother, and cleave to his wife; And they twain shall be one flesh: so then they are no more twain, but one flesh. What therefore God hath joined together, let not man put asunder. (Mark 10:7-9)

I am very proud of you and all that you do to help make up our family. I am proud to see you accomplish the publishing of your third book.

I remember you telling me, "I am going to write a book." I saw that come to pass.

I remember you telling me, "I am going to start my own business." I saw that come to pass. Everything you set out to do, you end up doing, with the help of the Lord. Both books have been a blessing to the people who have read them. So many testimonies came in concerning *Then and Now*. Many said they were healed and set free. I know Part II will also be a blessing to many.

You are a very strong woman that doesn't give up easily. I have seen you break down but you never gave up on God or lost your praise. I have seen God raise you back up. You always gave Him praise. I hear you praying and crying out to God on behalf of others. I can say you are and always have been a *true* woman of God. The Lord uses you in the word when you are preaching. Continue to let the Lord use you in everything you do and say. His anointing is upon you.

> Cry aloud, spare not, lift up thy voice like a trumpet, and shew my people their transgression, and the house of Jacob their sins. (Isaiah 58:1)

I thank God that you are the mother of my children. I thank God that we have learned how to hold each other up in times of trouble. I thank God for being married to you for thirty years and counting. I thank God for all that you had been through and all that I'd been through before we meet. God had you for me and me for you… He was waiting until we met.

I look forward to us growing old together and enjoying our grandchildren and great-grandchildren (if the Lord says the same). I thank God for all the things He has blessed us with. I thank God for all the things we went through. They only made us who we are today.

I don't know what I would do without you in my life. I love you so much. I am not good at writing. You know that. But… I am trying to say what I feel about you. I will always be "Big Daddy" and you will always be "Little Mommy". I love you.

Your husband and love
Dean

Chapter 10 • My Family and their Words

I don't know where to start… I guess I'll start by saying how proud I am of my mom. I thank God, every day, for my parents. I may not make it known or say it enough but I appreciate everything they have done for all of us. I thank God for using them as vessels in my life. I'm most thankful for the faith and wisdom they instilled in me.

I'm grateful for have praying parents. They showed me how to pray and to have faith to live according to His word. I have always been a blessed child. Because of the faith and hard work of my parents, I never really wanted for anything.

Growing up, I watched my mom be a blessing. She has carried God's word to different states and cities, telling how good He is. She has showed the world of His many wonders! Even now, I listen to tapes of her preaching.

I have truly been blessed to have her and my father in my life. I can't say it enough. I don't think I would even know God if it were not for them instilling the word of God in us. That, by far, has been the biggest gift they have given us. Don't get me wrong. The trips and Christmases were great. But, I don't know where I would be if it weren't for them leading me and teaching me right from wrong or how I should live. Oh, yes, they taught me to save money. They made me get a job. They made me get up early, even if I had nothing to do. Now, I see that all they taught me prepared me for adulthood. I'm forever grateful to my mother and father.

I can never really put into words how much they mean to me. I cannot express how greatly they have impacted my life. I might have gone off subject a little bit, but Mom, I'm proud of you. Congrats on your third book. The other two books were a blessing to me and everyone else who read them. Many testimonies came in from people who were hurt and abused. Many people have hurt and pain and never talk about it.

Mom, thank you for allowing the Lord to use you to help so many people. I thank you and Dad for always praying for me, regardless of what the situation was. You have given me something that no man can ever take away. I thank you so very much from my whole heart! You may not hear it enough, but I love you. May God continue to bless you and use you for His glory! I love you, Mom.

Your true "oldest"
Tawana

Momma, I was so excited when you wrote your first book. It has so many thrilling moments in it. It made me laugh, cry, and smile... all in one. I remember bringing you endless glasses of water when you were writing the first book. *Then and Now* has touched my heart and has been a great blessing to many.

I had to do a project for a college class. The whole class read *Then and Now* and was touched by it. One of my classmates was going through the same thing. The book touched her so much that she wrote a letter to my mother. My mother invited

Chapter 10 • My Family and their Words

her to church; talked with her; and led her to the Lord. My classmate gave her life to the Lord. I am excited to see all that this third book has to offer.

I enjoyed reading the second book, *Surviving Your Worst Fear*. When I was little, I had a fear of the dark and never wanted to be alone. The devil would fight me with that. My parents had to pray me through that until God brought me out.

I am so proud of my mother and all that she has accomplished: being a published author and owning her own businesses. I see her helping anyone she can. And… she will go out of her way to do it.

She always gave us everything we wanted. Of course, I was the one everyone called spoiled rotten. They said that I got even more than my other sisters. I never saw that (SMILE).

I am so proud of my mother. She taught me how to be the woman that I am. She always wanted us to be more than she ever was. She wanted us to have the best.

My father and mother *kept* us in church even when we didn't want to go.

She said, "You go get ready because you *are* going."

I can remember how my parents would come and pray for us even when we were asleep, "Bless them, Lord. Save them, Lord." I love to hear them preach the word of God.

I am studying toward my associate's degree. I would like to become a children's book author. I prayed that God would bless each and every one that reads my mother's books. I am blessed to have a mother and father like the ones the Lord gave us. I love them so much. I am thankful and blessed to have you as a mother. I love you so much.

Kenyatta, your second

I would like to start off by saying that I truly thank God for my mother. She is a loving, caring person who will go out of her way to try and make everyone happy and satisfied. As a child, my mom would teach us how to be women of God. Our parents had us in church every time the church doors opened.

I really, really love my mom. All I ever wanted was to just be her baby. I am so proud of my mom for all the books the Lord gave her to write and all the businesses they have.

Then and Now is a book I will never forget. My mom went through so much. For her to tell her story blessed me. I did cry *and* laugh. Now, she has written her third book. I can't wait to read it.

My mother taught me how to clean saying, "A man loves a clean house and some food in his belly." So, every time we had company in town, my mother would have me clean the house and tell me, "Get it good like I showed you. I know I can depend on you to do it."

Our parents always wanted us to have the best. We never had to worry about not having because our parents made sure we had everything: the latest styles and great vacations. We always went everywhere we wanted to go.

Chapter 10 ● My Family and their Words

You have blessed me with "love". I thank God that we are close. That is something I always wanted to be. I am so proud of both of my parents and all that they have been blessed with.

I'm 24 years old. I have a 6 month old son, Ivan, Jr. He is my parents' first – and only – grandchild. They always wanted a boy and my mom lost three boys. God has truly blessed me on my journey to being a mother. Mom, thank you for everything you taught us. As an adult, I have my own responsibilities. What you have taught me will help me carry them out well.

I got hired by Ford Motor Company in July. I will be continuing my life-long dream as a career. I love you, Mom, with all my heart.

Chantel, your third

My mom is a very strong woman. She has been through more than I could ever bear. My mom has accomplished a lot. One day, I plan to be able to say the same about myself. I'm so proud of her for completing her third book. I know it will be a blessing to many… just like the other two were. I enjoyed reading and helping her with her first book. It was a true blessing to everyone.

She has worked so hard and never gave up. Everything that she sets out to do gets done. All of her books are amazing. Sharing her stories helps others that have been through similar things. I believe sharing your personal life can actually be good because it can truly be a doorway for others to open up and relate. Her life story has been a blessing. It has brought healing to many people who have been abused and hurt.

Growing up, my mom always pulled us away from the life she had growing up. She wanted the best for us. We got the best, even though we thought she was just being hard on us. Now that I'm older, I can truly thank my mom for being so hard on some things. It made me a better person. It made me the woman I am today. I learned right from wrong from the things my mom told and taught me. I love and appreciate her for everything she has done for me and will do. I have the greatest parents on earth.

Mom, keep on letting the Lord use you and continue praying for us. I love you so much.

LaChisa, your baby girl

My daughter, Bonnie, is the most sweet, loving and giving person you can meet. I have known her since she came to IGC some thirty one years ago. I didn't get to know her like a daughter until I started traveling with her. We traveled from state to state as she preached the gospel to a dying generation. Many souls were saved, set free, healed, and delivered.

She had lost her natural mother and was looking for another mother, here on earth, to call Mom. The Lord was already using her. His anointing was upon her. She began to seek the Lord as never before, praying to God and telling him how

Chapter 10 • My Family and their Words

much she missed her natural mother. As we know, the Lord will meet every need.

> *Therefore I say unto you, What things so ever ye desire, when ye pray, believe that ye receive them, and ye shall have them.* (Mark 11:24)

He granted her prayer request and gave her me. Daughter Bonnie is just like a natural daughter to me. I love her as if she were my own. I thank God that He gave me to her.

The Lord has blessed her over and over again with much success. I never saw her get a big head. She never acted as though she was more than anyone else. Even after the Lord would use her greatly in all the revivals she preached, she stayed humble and faithful to God. As she went through many trials and tribulations, she never gave up her praise. She kept her praise and her faith. The Lord, Jesus, brought her out every time.

> *But He knoweth the way that I take: when He hath tried me, I shall come forth as gold.* (Job 23:10)

I see her going higher and higher in God as she keeps her little hands in God's big hands – as she has always done. She always says that the Lord is her shepherd and she shall not want. If it had not been for the Lord on her side where would she be today? I am so proud to be her Mom as she seeks the Lord and continues her walk in the Lord.

Daughter, Mom loves you
Mother Mary Jordon Meeks

About the Author

The Lord saved Bonnie in 1982 and filled her with the Holy Spirit on January 13, 1983. In 1985, she was called into the ministry. As she totally sold out to God, He blessed her with the gifts of intercession, discernment of spirits, prophecy and interpretation, the laying on of hands and the ministry of helps.

She has been a member of International Gospel Center for over thirty years. For the first fifteen years, she was under the leadership of the late Apostle Charles O. Miles and under the leadership of current Pastor Marvin N. Miles the last sixteen years. She is the supervisor of the Prayer Line Ministry, a Junior Pastor, an Evangelist, a Sunday School teacher for Children's Church, and a church nurse. She also faithfully serves in the intercessory prayer, nursing home and prison ministries.

Always a servant, Minister Baker works in the Spiritual Support Department of the local hospital. She ministers to as many as 60 patients a day, on every floor, including the Intensive Care Unit. She also consoles grieving families of patients who have passed away. She has led many patients and their family members to the Lord. Minister Baker recently ministered to a comatose patient. Tears began to fall from his eyes. Just after she finished ministering, he passed away. His sister testified,

"My brother found peace with God as a result of your ministry. He died with a smile on his face!"

During her Christian walk, Bonnie has received many visions and revelations from the Lord. She lives by the scriptures that say God will bless you coming in and going out and He will make you the head and not the tail.

The Lord has favored Bonnie with much success. She now owns her own mortgage company as well as a vending machine company, travel agency, online health store and natural health agency.

Bonnie has tasted everything the devil could serve up – yet her life has taken a 180-degree turn. She travels to various states, preaching the Word of God, declaring that Jesus saves and will save and free you if given the opportunity. Nothing is impossible with God if you allow Him into your heart.

Author Contact
Bonnie Baker
P. O. Box 74073
Romulus, MI 48174

Also available from Bonnie Baker

Then and Now
ISBN 978-1-56229-010-8
$14.99

Then and Now eBook
ISBN 978-1-56229-224-9
$9.99

Then and Now – Part 2 eBook
ISBN 978-1-56229-820-3
$9.99

Then and Now – Parts 1 and 2 Special Edition eBook
ISBN 978-1-56229-821-0
$15.99

Surviving Your Worst Fear
ISBN 978-1-56229-211-0
$9.99

Surviving Your Worst Fear eBook
ISBN 978-1-56229-225-6
$8.99

Available at ChristianLivingBooks.com or wherever books are sold.